# GUESS WHAT, GOD!

**PATRICIA A. SIMMONS**

BROADMAN PRESS  Nashville, Tennessee

© Copyright 1976 • Broadman Press
All rights reserved

4244-13
ISBN: 0-8054-4413-0

Dewey Decimal Classification: J242.2
Subject heading: DEVOTIONS, DAILY

Library of Congress Catalog Card Number: 75-22974
Printed in the United States of America

# 1

Having to make my bed every day is bad enough, God, and now they've added washing dishes and that's even worse! Dad always takes sides with Mom. "Whatever Mom says. Whatever Dad says." Boy, they stick together like glue. Well, as long as I have to do it, God, help me get it over with. Thanks for listening anyway.

**Whatever your task, work heartily, as serving the Lord and not men.** *Colossians 3:23*

# 2

Guess what, God! I had fun working today! I stacked all that wood for Dad, and he didn't even tell me to do it. Most of the time I don't like to work, but I guess sometimes it can be fun. The sun was so warm on my back, and the air smelled so good. Thanks for everything, God. Thanks especially for Dad's being so pleased with what I did.

**Pleasant sights and good reports give happiness and health.** *Proverbs 15:30*

# 3

Sunday School was fun today, God, except for memorizing those Bible verses. I don't know why we have to learn all that stuff. Thanks for the picnic and that it didn't rain. It was a pretty neat day.

> **Thy word have I hid in mine heart, that I might not sin against thee.** *Psalm 119:11*

# 4

God, I don't know how to say this, but when we go to that thing at school tomorrow night, would you please have Mom not hang around me. I want her to go, and I like her—I really do—but I just don't want to be with her. Maybe you could find some other mom for her to talk with. Thanks, God.

> **Love is very patient and kind.** *1 Corinthians 13:4*

# 5

Well, I blew it again, God. I got a *D* in English. I want to make good grades, but I don't like to study. I really do mean to do better and I start to study, but before I know what has happened my mind goes off somewhere else. Help me make my mind do what it should do, and help Mom and Dad not be too mad when they see my grades. And, also, would you make school hurry up and get out.

**To learn, you must want to be taught.** *Proverbs 12:1*

# 6

Tuck your shirttail in! Wash your elbows! Wash your ears! Comb your hair! I like my shirttail out because it is more comfortable. I comb my hair, and the wind messes it up again. You'd think I was getting ready for Sunday School every morning. I know being clean is part of staying healthy and all that jazz, but God, help Mom not to overdo it. Thanks.

**Create in me a new, clean heart, O God, filled with clean thoughts and right desires.** *Psalm 51:10*

# 7

God, I like my brother, but sometimes I don't like him, too. He always gets to do things with Dad because he is older. Sometimes I wish he was in my place. Sometimes I wish he wouldn't get to go anywhere at all. I wish I could go with Dad all by myself and my brother would have to stay home. He's so bossy and acts like a big know-it-all, and he doesn't know anymore than I do—not much more anyway. I'll be glad when it's my turn, God.

**Love is . . . never jealous or envious.** *1 Corinthians 13:4*

# 8

God, sometimes I get so mad at my little brother. He's always following me around and wanting to do everything I do. And what's more, he's a tattletale. He always runs to Mom saying, "Joe did this" or "Joe did that." I wish he'd grow up! Mom says some day we'll be surprised at how much we'll like each other. If that happens, I will be surprised. Help me to put up with him, God, since I'm stuck with him.

> **Love . . . is not irritable or touchy . . . and will hardly even notice when others do it wrong.** *1 Corinthians 13:5*

# 9

God, I like my grandma a lot, but could you keep her from hugging and kissing me when my friends are around? Maybe we could shake hands instead, and then she can kiss me after they've gone home. Thanks, God.

**Love bears all things . . . endures all things.** *1 Corinthians 13:7*

# 10

I hate football! I didn't want to play in the first place. Please, God, make Dad understand that I can't always like the same things he did. Give me the courage to tell him and the coach I don't want to play.

**Trust the Lord completely; don't ever trust yourself. In everything you do, put God first, and he will direct you.** *Proverbs 3:5-6*

## 11

God, I didn't mean to cry today when George and Powell were hurting that wild duck. I was so mad it just happened. I was so sorry for that duck, and I couldn't get them to leave it alone. I wish you'd make them stop being mean to animals, and I wish you'd help me figure out why it's OK for girls to cry and why I get called a sissy if I cry.

**Jesus wept.** *John 11:35*

# 12

Girls are sneaky, and sometimes I hate them, God. At least I hate Penny. How can you be a gentleman when girls do dumb things like turning your lightning bugs loose. If she were a boy, I'd be tempted to beat her up! Mom said she did it to make me notice her. Boy, I noticed her all right. Sometimes I wish you'd never made girls. I guess you'd better help me not to be so mad at her, and please help her think of some other way to make me notice her.

**Happy is the man who doesn't give in and do wrong when he is tempted.** *James 1:12*

# 13

I really like my grandpa. He treats me like I'm grown up, and he knows things that aren't in books. He knows how to recognize a bird by its wing spread. I learn more being quiet with him than I do by talking with most people. Look after him, God. Keep his back from hurting so much, and thanks for the time he shares with me.

**An old man's grandchildren are his crowning glory.**
*Proverbs 17:6*

# 14

This was a terrible day, God. I don't even know how that fight got started. I think Turk really likes to fight; but I sure don't—at least, not with my fists. Mom says words can hurt as much or more than fists. Please help me know how to get out of messes like this one today without being called chicken.

**It is hard to stop a quarrel once it starts, so don't let it begin.** *Proverbs 17:14*

# 15

Yippee! Thanks for the snow, God! Thanks for sleds and snowball fights and snow forts and hills to slide on and ice cream made out of snow! I think snow and Christmas and fires in fireplaces and holidays from school are the very best part of winter. Thanks for all of them, God.

**He sends the snow in all its lovely whiteness.** *Psalm 147:16*

# 16

You know, God, when Cooper and I are mad at each other I sure do feel awful inside. Mom said sometimes people got mad at you, too, when you hadn't hurt them or anything. Boy, I know just how you felt. Help me get to be friends with Cooper again. Thanks, God.

> **It is harder to win back the friendship of an offended brother than to capture a fortified city. His anger shuts you out like iron bars.** *Proverbs 18:19*

# 17

I don't like to take piano lessons, God. I don't like to practice. I don't like anything about it. I can't understand why Mom wants me to keep on. Please, please help me explain to her so she'll know how I feel. Help her try to see my side, and help us both not get mad at each other.

> **Each has his own special gift from God, one of one kind and one of another.** *1 Corinthians 7:7*

# 18

I don't think I will ever grow! I am so tired of being called "Half-pint" and "Shrimp" and all those other silly names. I think I'll slug the next one who calls me "Peewee." Please, God, help me keep my temper; and I wish I could really be a star at something where my size would be forgotten.

**God has given each of us the ability to do certain things well.** *Romans 12:6*

# 19

Please, God, when we go to the lake tomorrow, would you keep Dad from asking me to water-ski. And God, if I do have to ski, help me not to be so afraid. I'll bet Dad was never afraid to do anything. Maybe you could fix it so he would understand how I feel and keep it so he will still like me.

**Fear not, for I am with you. Do not be dismayed. I am your God. I will strengthen you; I will help you.** *Isaiah 41:10*

# 20

  I sure can't figure out girls! Sometimes I think I might like them, and then they come up with some dumb idea like wanting you to carry their books or asking to wear your ID bracelet. Why can't they wear their own bracelet and carry their own books? It's a good thing you made girls so they would turn into mothers or they wouldn't have been good for anything. Thanks for Mom and the cookies she made today.

> **There are . . . things too wonderful for me to understand . . . the growth of love between man and a girl.** *Proverbs 30:18-19*

# 21

Woodpeckers are fun to watch, God. You must have had a good time when you made the birds and animals. Monkeys that hang upside down, possums carrying babies on their tails, kangaroos with pockets, turtles that carry their houses with them. I don't see how you could have thought of so many different kinds, but I am glad you did. Thanks for all of them, Lord.

**O Lord, what a variety you have made! And in wisdom you have made them all! The earth is full of your riches.**
*Psalm 104:24*

# 22

Say, Lord, that team I have to pitch against has more than half their lineup with batting averages higher than all our team put together. I could sure use some help—kind of like the help you gave David when he went to meet Goliath. Don't let us get slaughtered, OK?

> **What is impossible with men is possible with God.** *Luke 18:27*

# 23

Thanks, God, for the good time Dad and I had this weekend. It was sure fun not having any women or girls around. Dad's not the best fisherman in the world, but we had fun anyway. I'm glad Dad is good at baseball, though; and besides, I guess you can't be good at everything.

> **God has given each of you some special abilities; be sure to use them to help each other, passing on to others God's many kinds of blessings.** *1 Peter 4:10*

# 24

Something funny happened today, God. You know how mad I was at my brother but on the way home from school when Cooper and Smith began bothering him, I didn't like it. That's kind of hard to figure out. I was mad at him until they started being mad at him, too; and then all of a sudden I was on his side. I guess I was mad at him and liking him at the same time. I wonder if you ever feel that way about people?

> **If you love someone you will be loyal to him no matter what the cost. You will always believe in him, always expect the best of him, and always stand your ground in defending him.** *1 Corinthians 13:7*

# 25

God, you know that game tonight. I know you care about both teams, and I know that prayers aren't supposed to be selfish. But, God, there's no way I can say I don't care which team wins because you know how much I want to win. Anyway, please help us all play our best and help us to be either good losers or good winners whichever way the game comes out; but I'd sure rather win if that's possible. Thanks a lot.

> **To win the contest you must deny yourself many things that would keep you from doing your best. An athlete goes to all this trouble just to win a blue ribbon or a silver cup, but we do it for a heavenly reward that never disappears.** *1 Corinthians 9:25*

# 26

Sisters are pests! I wish she would stay out of my room. She gets into everything and then ends up by getting me in trouble. Sometimes I wish she'd been a brother; then I could bust her one. I guess you probably wouldn't go for that, would you, God? Help me figure out something to do about her.

**Do for others what you want them to do for you. Matthew 7:12**

# 27

Hey, God, did you see Joe snitch that candy bar at the grocery store today? I didn't know whether to tell on him or not. I told him he had better put it back, but he just laughed and said he'd get a bigger one next time. He's got money, too, God. I like him, but would you make him not do stuff like that anymore. Thanks.

**If anyone is stealing he must stop it and begin using those hands of his for honest work.  Ephesians 4:28**

# 28

I sure blew everything, God. I don't know why I didn't tell Dad exactly how that window got broken. I didn't exactly lie, but I didn't exactly tell the truth either; so I guess it was more lie than truth. Everything went wrong from the minute I tried to get out of the blame. Next time help me to tell things like they happen, and then I won't have to worry about it. Thanks, God.

**What relief for those who have confessed their sins and God has cleared their record.** *Psalm 32:2*

# 29

Why did Pepper get killed, God? Something happens to every pet I get. I tried to take good care of Pepper. The neighbors let their pets run loose all the time and nothing ever happens to them. Some kids never have anything go wrong. It doesn't seem fair. This feeling inside of me is awful and it won't go away. Please, God, help me. And thanks for the good times I had with Pepper.

> **He maketh his sun to rise on the evil and on the good, and sendeth rain on the just and on the unjust.** *Matthew 5:45*

# 30

God, I don't think Dad and Mom are being fair. I wasn't that bad. I can't ride my bike for a whole week just because I went out of that dumb boundary line we set. Next time please help me remember to ask permission when I want to go somewhere on the other side of the boundary.

**Being punished isn't enjoyable while it is happening—it hurts! But afterwards we can see the result, a quiet growth in grace and character.** *Hebrews 12:11*

# 31

Hey, God, I sure had a great day! That cave was terrific. Thanks for the good time I had playing football. Thanks for the watermelon Dad brought home. Everything was fun today. Thanks a lot, God.

**When a man is . . . cheerful, everything seems right!** *Proverbs 15:15*

# 32

God, nobody seems to understand how I feel today. I don't think they even care. Mom wants me to do one thing, and Dad wants me to do something else. My sister is into my things. I wish everyone would let me alone and just let me be by myself. I don't even know why I feel this way, but please, God, make them understand.

**Jesus suggested, "Let's get away from the crowds for a while and rest."** *Mark 6:31*

# 33

God, Bill said I live in the cheapest house in the neighborhood. When I asked Dad if that was so, he said, "Probably." I like our house and besides, his mom won't let him have frogs in their kitchen. Thanks for our house, God, and for my frogs.

> **Don't live to make a good impression on others. Be humble, thinking of others as better than yourself.** *Philippians 2:3*

# 34

Oh, God, I've never felt so terrible in my whole life. I didn't mean to hurt anyone. I'll never, ever throw another rock as long as I live! I wasn't throwing at anyone. I was just throwing. You know I wasn't throwing at anyone. Please make them understand and know that I am sorry.

> If we confess our sins to him, he can be depended on to forgive us and to cleanse us from every wrong. *1 John 1:19*

# 35

Get in the wood. Rake the leaves. Sweep the garage. Do this. Do that. Will I ever be glad when I am grown up and away from all these orders. Sometimes I'd like to say, "I'm not going to do anything today." Sometimes I pretend a chunk of wood is my dad or my mom when I toss it on the wheelbarrow. Help me to get all this work done, and please don't let them think of anything else for me to do, at least not today.

**Idle hands are the devil's workshop.** *Proverbs 16:27*

# 36

I beat my dad at checkers tonight, God, and I didn't cheat and he didn't just let me beat him. Somehow it wasn't as much fun as I thought it would be. I think Dad was happier than I was. I wonder why I felt kind of sad about it? Was it because I only thought I wanted to win? Dad says you should always try to win but not be discouraged if you lose. Sometimes winning isn't as much fun as you think it will be.

> **In a race, everyone runs but only one person gets first prize. So run your race to win.** *1 Corinthians 9:24*

# 37

Thanks for bonfires, and hot dogs, and roasted marshmallows. I hope I don't get the stomachache tonight, God. Thanks for the hayride and the good time we had. I wonder what the kids in the big cities do for fun. I hope they have a good time, too. I'm glad I live where I do, God.

**I will sing to the Lord because he has blessed me so richly.** *Psalm 13:6*

# 38

God, you know my friend, Bob. I am sorry his dad had to die. Bob gets real mad if anyone even mentions his dad. I think he pretends to be mad so he won't cry. He likes my dad a lot. Thanks for my dad; and God, could you maybe help Bob when he needs a dad? Thanks.

**Father of the fatherless . . . is God in his holy habitation.** *Psalm 68:5*

# 39

God, I can't figure out why some babies have to be born crippled. If a person gets sick or has an accident that causes him to be crippled, I can understand that; but it doesn't seem fair for a baby to be born that way. Mom says you never promised life would be fair, but I still can't figure some things out. Anyway, thanks that I am healthy; and will you please be with those guys who can't run and play ball and things like that.

**Trust in the Lord with all your heart, and do not rely on your own insight.** *Proverbs 3:5*

# 40

I like going barefoot and feeling the warm ground under my feet. I like rain, too, and the way my toes feel when mud squishes between them. Did you ever look at a rainbow in a puddle of water after a rain? I even like to walk in the rain and feel it on my face. The air always smells so fresh and clean after it has rained. You really did a pretty neat job when you made the world, God. Thanks for it.

**And God saw every thing that he had made, and, behold, it was very good.** *Genesis 1:31*

# 41

You know ants are fun to watch, God. I tried to sidetrack those ants today to get them away from their ant hill, but they always found their way back. They sure do hurry all the time, and that one had a load three times bigger than he was. I'm glad you made the ants, God, except next time would you please keep them out of our picnic basket. Thanks.

> **Take a lesson from the ants. . . . Learn from their ways and be wise!** *Proverbs 6:6*

# 42

More than anything, God, I want to play baseball when I grow up. I want to pitch in the All-Star game and in the World Series. Thanks for Dad taking me to the All-Star game and for the good time we had. Thanks for baseball.

> **So don't be anxious about tomorrow. God will take care of your tomorrow too. Live one day at a time.** *Matthew 6:34*

# 43

Get your elbows off the table. Chew with your mouth closed. Use your napkin. Don't eat so fast. It's hard to remember all that junk, especially when you're hungry. Dogs sure are lucky. Nobody hollers at them about their manners. Would you help Mom not to notice so much and help me to remember at least some of that stuff.

> **Do all things without grumbling or questioning.** *Philippians 2:14*

# 44

Lord, I think trouble just follows me around. Everything I've done today has gone wrong. I hope you forgive quicker than Dad and Mom. Sometimes it seems they really harp on things I do wrong. I wish you'd help them stop this and help me stay out of trouble.

**Your heavenly Father will forgive you if you forgive those who sin against you; but if you refuse to forgive them, he will not forgive you.** *Matthew 6:14-15*

# 45

Sometimes, God, I think of you as being like the wind. I can't see the wind or touch it, but I can see what it does. The wind touches me even though I can't touch it. Sometimes when I'm sad and I think about you, I get to feeling better like maybe you had touched me. Thanks, God.

**Just as you can hear the wind but can't tell where it comes from or where it will go next, so it is with the Spirit.** *John 3:8*

# 46

Thanks, God, for my getting to help with the TV sports broadcast. But you know after I got home, Tom called me a show-off and told me to stay out of his yard. I thought he was my friend. It seems like when bad things happen to you everybody comes to say they are sorry, but when something good happens about the only ones who are happy with you are your family. Help me to be happy for my friends when something good happens to them.

> **When others are happy, be happy with them. If they are sad, share their sorrow.** *Romans 12:15*

# 47

    I'll be glad when I get old enough to get a job besides mowing yards. I know it is wrong to hate, but I think I hate Mrs. Burge. She's the pickiest person I know and also the grouchiest. I don't think she ever smiles. If we were in the desert and she was the only one with water, I'll bet she wouldn't share. Help me get her yard mowed to please her, and help me not lose my temper, and keep me from hating her.

**Get rid of your feelings of hatred.** *1 Peter 2:1*

# 48

God, most of the time I really like collecting for my paper route, but why doesn't Mrs. Jones ever have the money to pay for her paper? She seems to have money for everything else. Please have her answer the door today and have her have the money to pay for her paper so I don't have to go back forty times. Thanks.

> **We can rejoice, too, when we run into problems and trials for we know they are good for us—they help us learn to be patient.** *Romans 5:3*

# 49

Thanks a lot for the good time I had today, God. You know sometimes it's not bad at all having a brother. You always have someone to play with. And you've always got somebody to stick up for you if you get picked on. Thanks for the fish we caught, God.

**A brother is born to help in time of need.** *Proverbs 17:17*

# 50

Being sick isn't any fun—being really sick I mean. Sometimes when you are not quite well enough to go to school, that's all right; but I sure do hate throwing up. I'm glad Mom is here when I am sick. Thanks, God, for letting me be well most of the time; and thanks for Mom.

**For I will restore health to you . . . says the Lord.** *Jeremiah 30:17*

# 51

God, I'm going deer hunting with Dad tomorrow. I like going out in the woods, and I like seeing wild animals running free. I don't want to tell Dad, but I sure hope we don't see any deer tomorrow. It would be like shooting at Bambi. I wouldn't want to see a deer die. Please keep them safe tomorrow. Thanks, God.

> **For everything there is a season, and a time for every matter under heaven: a time to be born, and a time to die.** *Ecclesiastes 3:1-2*

## 52

Lord, I don't want to go to camp. I don't like to stay away from home, and I don't like to do the things they do at camp. Help Dad and Mother understand this, and help me make them understand why I don't want to go. Just thinking about it makes me feel like I'm going to throw up. I like to stay with Grandpa and Grandma. Maybe I could go visit them. Please help me.

**Show me the path where I should go, O Lord; point out the right road for me to walk.** *Psalm 25:4*

# 53

I'm glad I can talk to you, God. I asked Cooper if he ever prayed, and he said he didn't believe in stuff like that. You know what I think, God? I think he does, but he just won't admit it. Sometimes it seems like he doesn't want anyone to know he does things that are good. I like him, God; and I'm glad he's my friend.

**When you pray, go away by yourself, all alone, and shut the door behind you and pray to your Father secretly, and your Father, who knows your secrets, will reward you.** *Matthew 6:6*

# 54

Man, did I get into trouble today, but it was worth it, God! You should have heard tattletale Patty scream when all those grasshoppers jumped out of her pencil box. I can't see how you could ever like somebody like her. I'll bet her own mother doesn't like her. I'm sorry I did something you don't like me to do, but it's hard to understand why you'd want me to like someone like her.

**If you are friendly only to your friends, how are you different from anyone else? Even the heathen do that.**
*Matthew 5:47*

## 55

Lord, I'd sure like to know why you ever made a thing like chicken pox. I'll bet if you ever had them, you'd do a miracle and get rid of them forever. They are the itchiest things in the whole world. Well, since we have the chicken pox, I'm glad you made baking soda and that other medicine Mom uses. I wish you'd please help these things not itch so much, and help me find something to do so I won't think about how much it itches. Thanks.

**Give thanks in all circumstances; for this is the will of God in Christ Jesus for you.** *1 Thessalonians 5:18*

# 56

God, I'm so mad at Dad I don't even like him! Jeff got his minibike today. I guess I'll never get one. There's just no way Dad's going to change his mind. I can tell. It seems like everything I want is either too dangerous, too expensive, or too something. I'll sure be glad when I have my own money to spend and can make up my own mind.

**The selfish man quarrels against every sound principle of conduct by demanding his own way.** *Proverbs 18:1*

# 57

God, sometimes I wonder who decided which were good words and which were bad words. When I'm mad, words just pop out before I know it. Burksey really swears a lot whether he is mad or not. I know the Bible tells us to say just yes or no, but sometimes that's hard to do. I wish you'd help me think first before I say anything. Thanks, God.

> **But most of all, dear brothers, do not swear either by heaven or earth or anything else; just say a simple yes or no, so that you will not sin and be condemned for it.** *James 5:12*

# 58

I wish I didn't have to go to bed so early. Everyone stays out later than I do. I wish you'd help Mom and Dad understand that I am not a baby anymore. Help them understand how much I want to do this. Maybe we could just try it for a week and see how it works.

**The wisdom that comes from heaven . . . allows discussion and is willing to yield to others.** *James 3:17*

# 59

"My, my, what beautiful hair! You are too pretty to be a boy. You should have been a girl!" I am not a girl! I am a boy! And, Lord, if that woman says that to me one more time, I think I'll explode. If she is in the store today, help me see her first so I can get away. Thanks, God.

**It is better to have self-control than to control an army.**
*Proverbs 16:32*

# 60

Today I shot a squirrel with my new rifle. Dad said it was really a good shot. I kind of hated it when the squirrel fell, but Mom is cooking it for dinner so maybe it isn't worse than buying meat in the grocery store. Sometimes I have a hard time figuring out things like this, God.

> **A lazy man won't even dress the game he gets while hunting, but the diligent man makes good use of everything he finds.** *Proverbs 12:27*

# 61

Thanks God, for the ribbons I won at the fair. Thanks for the fair and the happy feeling inside of me. I'd like to tell the whole world about winning, but I know I can't do that. Dad says it's OK to feel good about something like that when you have worked hard for it. Thank you that I can tell Grandpa about it.

> **Don't praise yourself; let others do it.** *Proverbs 27:2*

# 62

I like attics, God, especially when they are full of lots of junk. I like to look at the funny things that are packed away in boxes and trunks. You know—the things that were used in the olden times when Mom and Dad were little. Boy, I guess it was really a long time ago when Grandpa and Grandma were little. There is even stuff in the attic that belonged to them! Thanks for the good time my sister and I had in the attic today.

> **Lord, help me to realize how brief my time on earth will be.** *Psalm 39:4*

# 63

Say, God, the next time you see Moses would you tell him a lady down here compared him to an astronaut. I thought she was square until I started thinking about how Moses probably didn't know much about the country where he was going and the astronauts didn't know much about the moon either. Moses asked you to help him, and the astronauts prayed, too. Boy, I'd of prayed a lot if I had been either one of them. Thanks for helping us when we pray.

> **If you abide in me, and my words abide in you, ask whatever you will, and it shall be done for you.** *John 15:7*

# 64

Hey, God, did you see how many frogs I caught today? I'll bet I got forty at least! They sure are fun to catch. We are going to have a frog jumping contest at Scouts, and then Mom says we have to take them back to the pond and turn them loose. Turtle races are fun, too; but I couldn't find enough turtles. Thanks for frogs, God, and for turtles.

**A good man is concerned for the welfare of his animals.**
*Proverbs 12:10*

# 65

God, I have the best teacher in the whole world—and she is also the prettiest. She doesn't yell when you make a mistake, and she doesn't wad up your paper and throw it in the trash and make you start over like that old witch did last year. She didn't even get mad when Tom threw the paper wad and missed the wastebasket. She just said: "You'll never make the team that way. Next time dunk it." Thanks a lot for this teacher.

**A wise teacher makes learning a joy.** *Proverbs 15:2*

# 66

I nearly choked to death today, God! I guess you already know about those cigarettes. Man, I don't know how people can like something that tastes so terrible—it was worse than spinach. Next time, God, give me the courage to tell the guys, "Thanks, but no thanks!"

> **If young toughs tell you, "Come and join us"—turn your back on them.** *Proverbs 1:10*

# 67

God, when there is an argument going on in our yard, would you please keep Dad in the house. I know he wants to help; but when he comes out, he usually just makes things worse. Help me explain to Dad that we can work things out if he will let us, and help him understand that if I need him, I will call him. Thanks, God.

> **Blessed are the peacemakers: for they shall be called the children of God.** *Matthew 5:9*

# 68

Steve is a big bully, Lord. At recess he picks out somebody and tells them he is going to beat them up on the way home from school. Today he picked me, and I was really scared! If somebody bigger would come along and beat the tar out of him, maybe he would quit; but I guess you wouldn't like that, would you? Anyway, thanks a lot for helping me outrun him, and would you see if you can get him something to do besides beating up on somebody?

**Don't repay evil for evil. Wait for the Lord to handle the matter.** *Proverbs 20:22*

# 69

God, you know that little voice inside that talks to me? Sometimes I get mad when it won't be quiet, and then sometimes I wonder if it's your way of telling me to do or not to do something. I know it's called conscience, but it's kind of like a radio sending out warning signals to help keep me out of trouble. I guess it's a good thing you gave me one, and would you please help me pay more attention to the signals I get. Thanks.

**A man's conscience is the Lord's searchlight exposing his hidden motives.** *Proverbs 20:27*

# 70

Today when we left for our picnic I was so happy, God; but then I saw Phil and Burt standing in their driveway watching us pack the car. It made me feel kind of sad, because they don't get to go on picnics and do things like we do. They always have to stay home while their parents go places. Sometimes I think their dad doesn't even like them the way he yells at them. Maybe we can take them to the fair with us next week, God. Thanks for the picnic.

**Let us stop just saying we love people; let us really love them, and show it by our actions.** *1 John 3:18*

# 71

Lord, if I told Dick that Dad gave Mom the Hope Diamond, he'd say his dad gave his mom something bigger and better. If I hit one home run, he says he has hit two. If I do fifty sit-ups, he's done sixty. Most of the time you can tell what he is saying isn't true, so why does he say it? I wish he'd quit bragging—especially about the stuff he makes up. Help me remember not to boast about things, and help me be nice to Dick even when I get mad at him.

**If anyone is going to boast, let him boast only of what the Lord has done.** *1 Corinthians 1:31*

# 72

God, I'm so mad at that knothead, Joe, I don't think I'll ever get over being mad at him! When I get something he doesn't have, why does he always try to break it? Today he bent the spokes of my new ten-speed by pushing that stick through the wheel and then said it was an accident. He knew it wasn't an accident. He did it on purpose. He was just mad because I got a new bike before he did. Please help me not be envious of what my friends have, and please keep Joe out of my way for a few days until I get over being mad at him.

> **How often should I forgive a brother who sins against me? Seven times? "No," Jesus replied, "seventy times seven!"** *Matthew 18:21-22*

# 73

Speck isn't any special kind of dog, God, except for being special because I love him. Why does that show-off, Melinda, think dogs aren't any good if they don't have a pedigree. I wouldn't swap my dog for a hundred thousand dollars to get a dog with one of those things. I even feel sorry for her dog, God, because I'll bet she never lets him swim in the pond or anything. Thanks for Speck.

**Be satisfied with what you have.** *Hebrews 13:5*

# 74

God, I wonder if kids who live in the country wish they could live in the city. I wish I could have animals for pets and go fishing and hunting and do all those things I can't do. Even my grandparents live in the city. Maybe you could find me a new friend, God, who has grandparents in the country and then he could invite me to go visit them. Well, at any rate, it's fun to go to the zoo and do things like that. Thanks, God.

> **A bird in the hand is worth two in the bush; mere dreaming of nice things is foolish; it's chasing the wind.**
> *Ecclesiastes 6:9*